Ferocious Girls,
STEAMROLLER BOYS,
and Other Poems In Between

Ferocious Girls,
STEAMROLLER BOYS,

and Other Poems In Between

written and illustrated by

TIMOTHY BUSH

Orchard Books ▪ New York

Orchard Books
A Grolier Company
95 Madison Avenue
New York, NY 10016

Manufactured in the United States of America
Printed and bound by Phoenix Color Corp.
Book design by Kristina Albertson
The text of this book is set in 15 point Meridian.
The illustrations are watercolor.

10 9 8 7 6 5 4 3 2 1

Library of Congress Cataloging-in-Publication Data
Bush, Timothy.
Ferocious girls, steamroller boys, and other poems in between /
by Timothy Bush. p. cm.   Summary: Poems about people and
events commonly encountered in a child's life.
ISBN 0-531-30250-4 (trade : alk. paper).—
ISBN 0-531-33250-0 (lib. bdg. : alk. paper)
1. Children's poetry, American.   [1. American poetry.]
I. Title. PS3552.U8218F47   2000   811'.54—dc21   99-31532

For Helen and Jack

Ferocious Girls

The woods are full of girls today,
The big ferocious kind,
So I will not be going out—
I hope that you don't mind.

Ferocious girls do not play fair;
They call you names, they pull your hair.
Ferocious girls will eat your lunch.
Ferocious girls can take a punch.
Karate chop 'em? Doesn't stop 'em!
BIG FEROCIOUS GIRLS.

Ferocious girls are everywhere:
They're lurking in the trees,
They're crouching 'round the bend to pounce
On unsuspecting you's and me's.

They'll grab you with their fearsome claws.
They'll chomp you with tremendous jaws.
They'll grind your bones to make their bread.
They'll practice hockey with your head.
They'll beat you up! They'll kill you dead!
Those BIG FEROCIOUS GIRLS.

The girls start out in twos and threes
And then start forming packs,
And there is no place you can run
When one of those attacks.

The woods are full of girls today,
And going out just wouldn't pay.
So here I am and here I'll stay.
I will not budge: no how, no way!
There's really nothing you can say
But oh! . . .

MY KITE

Me and my kite

Are having a fight;

It's   *trying*   *to*

drag   *me*   *away.*

That is to say

My kite and I

Disagree

On who should be

Up   in   the

sky.

Aunt Mae

Our Aunt Mae

Likes to join us when we play.

We rather that she didn't

But she does it anyway.

Meow?

Whenever we play zoo
Mae will never do
What the animal she wants to be
Might be expected to.

She plays the walrus tropical,
She plays the lion shy.
She says she's an electric eel,
Then won't electrify.

She says that she's an elephant,
Then claims that she can fly.
Her mouse was so ferocious
That it made my cousin cry.

We tell Mae

"Will you please just go away?"

She always tells us

"Yes, I will!"

. . .And then proceeds to stay.

Go, Go, Go!

Go, **Go,**

Go!

I like to

PARK

Fly,

Fly.

I fly inside,

outside,

upside down

Over the rooftops into town.

Uncle Irving, we have heard
Believes himself to be a bird
And nothing anybody tries
Can quite convince him otherwise.

In spite of Mother's firm request
He's gone and built himself a nest
And sleeps—although we're not sure how
While clinging to the highest bough.

The neighbors called reporters in

And Grandpa called the looney bin

And folks from every part of town
Come to coax my uncle down.

But Uncle Irving doesn't care—

He continues sitting there.

And if he ever moves at all

It will be south,

and in the fall.

Adventure Dog

I like to watch Adventure Dog
I watch him every day
While all the other kids I know
Go run around and play.

Adventure Dog is wonderful
Adventure Dog is cool
I'd rather watch Adventure Dog
Than eat or go to school.

I memorize the episodes
I buy the toys and stuff
A houseful of Adventure Dog
Would still not be enough.

I play his games, I read his books
I sleep between his sheets
I wear his T-shirts and I eat
Adventure Doggie Treats.

I never want to drive a car
Or take an airplane ride
Or marry, visit Paris
. . . I won't even go outside.

I can't imagine anything
I'd rather do or be
I can't imagine anything
That's not on my TV.

Oh, no! My head has become a
television set and my face is now
just a picture on a screen!

STEAMROLLER BOYS

Maybe they're born that way.

Maybe they learn it.

Maybe it's bright morning sunshine that does it.
No one can really explain why it happens;
Medical science can't *why* or *because* it.

But although they may climb out of bed every day
Looking like perfect and heavenly joys
A strange transformation takes place after breakfast
And angels are changed . . .

. . . into steamroller boys.

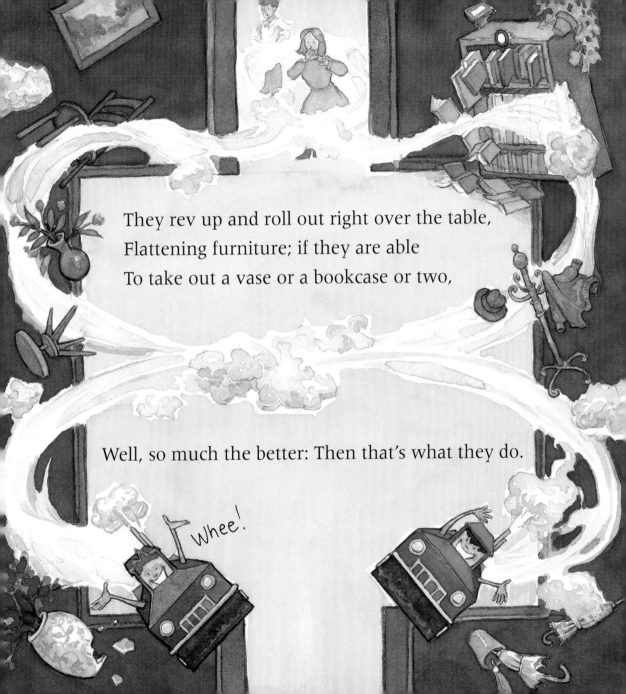

They rev up and roll out right over the table,
Flattening furniture; if they are able
To take out a vase or a bookcase or two,

Well, so much the better: Then that's what they do.

Whee!

Then over the lawn, then away down the street
Where steamroller boys by the dozen can meet:

There's Brian and Ryan! There's William and Bill!
There's Scotty and Spotty and Stinky and Gil!

And once they get going, the hullabaloo
Is seven-eighths riot and one-quarter zoo.
The crashing! The clashing! The clanking! The noise
Is sweeter than music to steamroller boys!

They race about steamrolling all that they see
And sensible people will pick up and flee.
The steamroller boys may not mean any harm,
But if you're not careful, you might lose an arm.

But after they've flattened the last of the grass,
One by one, steamrollers run out of gas.
They nod and they slump and they stumble and yawn
And stretch themselves out on the wreck of the lawn.

Then the people who fled all come back, one by one.
What a mess has been made by the boys and their fun!
The trees have been bent and the fence is destroyed;
The garden's a ruin. The birds are annoyed.

But the small sleepy faces are happy from play,
So the people all shrug, and then smile and say:
"The grass will grow back. It has grown back before.
And if not for the kids, well then what's a yard for?"

Then all of the people, though shaking their heads,
Carry boys home to their steamroller beds,

Where steamroller boys will all slumber away
And dream of another big steamroller day.